Walt Disney: 84 Fascinating Facts For Kids

Colin Mitchell

This book is just one of a series of "Fascinating Facts For Kids" books. For more fascinating facts about people, history, animals, and much more please visit:

www.fascinatingfactsforkids.com

Contents

Introduction

From humble beginnings in Chicago, Walt Disney was to become one of the most famous and successful Americans of all time.

Through hard work, determination, and vision, he survived bankruptcy and hard times, and went on to revolutionize the family entertainment industry, not just in the United States, but throughout the world.

He brought us iconic cartoon characters like "Mickey Mouse," "Snow White," and "Donald Duck," as well as classic movies such as "Mary Poppins" and "1001 Dalmatians," winning a record twenty-two Oscars along the way.

Walt Disney wasn't perfect - he had his faults like everyone else, but he was a remarkable man whose movies and theme parks have entertained and enchanted millions of children and adults for decades.

I hope the following facts will fascinate you and encourage you to find out even more about Walt Disney.

Colin Mitchell
November 2014

Early Life

1. Walter Elias Disney was born in Chicago, Illinois, on December 5, 1901, the fourth of Elias and Flora Disney's five children.

2. Walter's name was shortened to "Walt" by his nine-year-old brother, Roy.

3. Elias Disney was a stern and bad-tempered father, and Walt and his brothers and sister were scared of him. But his mother, Flora, was just the opposite in character - she was a warm-hearted and friendly woman who enjoyed laughing and playing with her children.

Flora & Elias Disney

4. Back in the early twentieth century, Chicago was becoming more and more violent and lawless, so the Disney family decided to move away to a more peaceful location. In 1906, they bought a farm in the small town of Marceline, Missouri, where Walt was to spend the happiest days of his childhood.

5. It was in Marceline that Walt drew his first pictures, sketching the animals on the farm and in the surrounding fields. Because of the scarcity of paper at the time, Walt's earliest pictures were drawn on toilet paper!

6. His favorite animal on the farm was a large pig named "Porker," which Walt used to ride around on as if it were a horse. He was regularly tossed into the farm pond!

7. The local doctor got to see some of Walt's drawings and asked him to draw a picture of Rupert, his magnificent stallion. The doctor gave Walt fifty cents for the finished picture, the first time he made money from his drawing!

8. Times were hard in Marceline, though, following two years of crop failure and an outbreak of swine fever, and when Walt's father became too ill to work on the farm the family decided to sell up and move to the city.

9. In 1910, after Walt and his brothers had finished their schooling, the Disney family moved to Kansas City. Here, his father's health improved but the failure of his farm had made his temper even worse.

1. Vermont
2. New Hampshire
3. Massachusetts
4. Rhode Island
5. Connecticut
6. New Jersey
7. Delaware
8. Maryland

Kansas

10. In Kansas, Walt's father took over a newspaper delivery business, and he employed ten-year-old Walt and his brother, Roy, as delivery boys. They had to get up at 3.15 every morning to deliver newspapers before school, and there were more deliveries after school as well as at weekends.

Walt the newsboy (bottom row - right)

11. Walt did not get paid by his father, who insisted he was investing his wages for him, so to earn pocket money he took a job in a candy store outside of school hours. Walt loved sweets, so this job enabled him to satisfy his sweet tooth as well as earn some money!

12.   The money Walt earned at the candy store allowed him to set up his own newspaper delivery business, which meant he now had to get out of bed at 3.00 in the morning to do two newspaper rounds!

13.   Walt enjoyed earning money, but he also enjoyed drawing. He was talented, and decided he wanted to earn his living by drawing. His father thought this foolish and said he would be better off learning a musical instrument if he wanted to do something artistic. He was forced to practice the violin for hours every day and hated every minute.

14.   It was in Kansas that Walt became friendly with a classmate who introduced him to the world of silent movies, which fascinated him.

15.   He and his sister, Ruth, also became regular visitors to the nearby amusement park, which never failed to enchant and delight them.

16.   It was also at this time that Walt developed his life-long love of trains. When he was fifteen years old he got a summer job working on the Pacific Railroad, selling newspapers to passengers. To his great delight, he was sometimes even allowed to ride in the coal car!

Chicago Again

17. In 1917, Elias Disney decided to sell the newspaper business and move back to Chicago where he had invested in a jelly-making company. It was thought best not to interrupt Walt's education, so he was to stay on in Kansas City and join his parents when he had taken his school exams. Walt was delighted with this arrangement, as he could continue his newspaper round and not have to suffer his father's temper.

18. Walt began his final year of school in Chicago at McKinley High School, where he drew cartoons for the school magazine.

McKinley High School

19. He decided to improve his drawing skills by enrolling as a night student at the Chicago Academy of Fine Arts, where he impressed his teacher with caricatures of animals.

20. To pay the fees at the Academy, Walt took jobs on Chicago's elevated railway and at the Post Office.

21. World War One was going on at this time, and Walt was eager to go to Europe to fight for his country. He was rejected by the Army but was recruited as an ambulance driver by the Red Cross. He sailed for France in October 1918.

Walt Disney the ambulance driver

22. The war was all but over by then and Walt missed any fighting, but for a sixteen-year-old it was exciting to see the world outside of Chicago and Kansas City.

Walt and Ub

23. On returning from France, Elias Disney tried to persuade Walt to accept a job at the jelly-making factory in Chicago, but Walt turned it down, insisting that he was going to earn a living as an artist.

24. Walt returned to Kansas City to live with his older brother, Roy, and set about finding employment.

25. He found a job as a temporary apprentice at the Pesmen-Rubin Art Studio where he drew illustrations for advertisements, for which he was paid $12 a week.

26. It was at Pesmen-Rubin that he met another cartoonist by the name of Ub Iwerks, who was to play a major role in Walt's future success.

27. Ub taught Walt many professional drawing techniques, and when his apprenticeship came to an end after two months, Walt was confident of earning a living as a commercial artist.

28. Ub's employment had also come to an end with Pesmen-Rubin, and the two young men decided to set up in business together.

29.   Walt and Ub were complete opposites in character, and the happy-go-lucky Walt often upset Ub with thoughtless teasing and practical jokes.

30.   The first office of "Iwerks & Disney, Commercial Artists" was a spare bathroom in downtown Kansas City!

31.   Although Ub was a brilliant illustrator, he was a hopeless salesman, so it was left to Walt to find paying clients - which he did with some success. It wasn't long before the partners were able to move out of their spare bathroom and into a proper office!

32.   For some time, both Walt and Ub had been fascinated by the cartoons that were showing at the local movie houses, and were intrigued by the appearance of an advertisement for the post of cartoonist at the Kansas City Film Ad Company.

33.   Walt took examples of his work to the Film Ad Company and was offered the post there and then. Walt and Ub had hoped that they could both share the work, but Walt was told that the job was for one person only.

34.   The two men agreed that Walt should take the job and hand over his share of "Iwerks & Disney" to Ub, who would run the business on his own.

35. Secretly, Walt was glad to be rid of his partner who had become something of a burden. Ub, though, had been resentful towards Walt for some time because of the teasing and practical jokes.

Partnership Restored

36. Walt's fascination with animated cartoons grew and grew. He read every book he could find on the subject and went to the movies at least five times a week.

37. He was convinced that the cartoons of the day could be of a much higher quality, but he was also aware of the limitations of his drawing techniques. Ub Iwerks was a much better artist than Walt, who realized he needed his former partner back if he was going to make the cartoons he dreamed of making.

38. Ub had been a disaster at running "Iwerks & Disney" and the company went bankrupt. This gave Walt the opportunity to get them both back together.

39. The twenty-year-old Walt was full of ideas and energy, and after borrowing a film camera from the Film Ad Company he made a series of "Laugh-O-Grams," which were shown in movie houses across Kansas City.

40. These "Laugh-O-Gram" cartoons were such a success that Walt resigned from the Film Ad Company to set up his own production company, "Laugh-O-Gram Films, Inc."

41.   He made two short films, "Puss in Boots" and "Red Riding Hood," featuring both live actors and cartoon characters, that were shown on movie screens across the country.

42.   His next project was much more ambitious, a film based on a story by Lewis Carroll called "Alice's Wonderland," which starred a real-life Alice surrounded by cartoon animals.

43.   Despite these early successes, "Laugh-O-Gram Films" was a financial disaster, and Walt was forced to go bankrupt in 1923.

To Hollywood

44. Despite the failure of "Laugh-O-Gram Films" Walt was still full of ambition, and in July 1923, aged twenty-two and with $50 in his pocket, he boarded a train which was bound for Hollywood.

45. Walt met up with his brother Roy in California, and persuaded him to become his business partner. They formed the "Disney Brothers Studio" to make cartoon movies.

46. Their first cartoon was "Alice's Day at the Sea," which was the first in a series of movies that Walt was to make based on Lewis Carroll's character from "Alice in Wonderland."

47. One criticism of Walt's movies was the quality of Walt's drawings. He accepted this criticism and realised that he had to get his old partner, Ub Iwerks, to work for him again.

48.   Ub agreed to come to California and started work at the Disney Brothers Studio on a salary of $40 a week.

49.   Walt's "Alice" films now started to get rave reviews and began to make money, which could be invested in more ambitious projects.

50.   Walt and Ub were commissioned to produce a series of animated films, and they came up with a cartoon character called "Oswald the Lucky Rabbit."

51.   The "Oswald" cartoons were a great success, but when Walt lost the rights for the character he was determined to replace him with something just as good. On a long train journey from New York to Hollywood, Walt was sketching away and came up with the idea of one of the most famous cartoon characters ever.

Mickey Mouse

52.   In 1925, Walt had married Lillian Bounds, whom he had hired to ink in his sketches. When he showed her drawings of his new character, "Mortimer Mouse," she said it sounded too pompous and suggested "Mickey" instead.

53.   Walt and Ub developed a character for Mickey Mouse. He would be mischievous, impudent, and always getting into trouble when helping people out.

54.   The first Mickey Mouse film, "Plane Crazy" came out in 1928, and was followed by "Galopin' Gaucho." Both received lukewarm receptions.

55.   It was the third film, "Steamboat Willie," the first ever cartoon to feature sound, that really took off, making Mickey Mouse a household name both in the United States and abroad.

56.   Walt himself provided the voice for Mickey Mouse, and all his films in the future were to have soundtracks.

Success After Success

57. Walt made many more Mickey Mouse cartoons, but also experimented with other ideas. He began the "Silly Symphonies" series of cartoons, and introduced new characters including "Minnie Mouse," "Donald Duck," "Pluto," and "Goofy."

58. "Flowers and Trees," which was released in 1932, was the first cartoon to be filmed in color, and was also the first cartoon to win an Academy Award. Walt was on his way to becoming one of the most successful movie makers of all time.

59. While the Disney Brothers Studio went from strength to strength, Walt suffered a setback when Ub left the company, but more animators were hired to bring his ideas to life.

60. Disney was always trying out new things and he now wanted to make a feature-length animated film.

61. Many of Walt's colleagues, including his brother, Roy, were worried about the time and money needed to make a full-length movie, but Walt was determined, and chose the story of "Snow White" for his first feature-length cartoon.

62. "Snow White and the Seven Dwarfs" took two years to make and was premiered in December 1937. It received a standing ovation from a star-studded audience.

63. "Snow White" made money not just from the box office, but also through the sale of related merchandise. Millions of replicas of the Seven Dwarfs were made and sold all over the world.

64. When somebody wins an Academy Award, they are presented with an "Oscar" - a thirteen-and-a-half-inch (34 cm) high statuette. When "Snow White" won an Oscar, Walt was also presented with seven miniature statuettes to represent the Seven Dwarfs!

Walt Disney & the Seven Dwarfs

Setbacks and a Strike

65. Three more full-length cartoons followed – "Pinocchio," "Fantasia," and "Bambi," but none could match the success of "Snow White." They may have been too far ahead of their time for the audiences of the day.

66. "Fantasia" was developed from the "Silly Symphonies" films, and featured music from classical composers such as Beethoven, Tchaikovsky, and Stravinsky.

67. "Fantasia" was Disney's most expensive movie so far, costing over $2,000,000 to make, of which $500,000 was spent on the music alone.

68. Because of the relative failure of these three films, and the fact that the market for them in Europe had dried up because of World War Two, the profits from "Snow White" had disappeared.

69. The Disney Studio was now in financial trouble, and Roy and Walt decided that they had to cut the wages of their hundreds of employees.

70. On hearing about the plans to cut their wages, the workers went on strike, refusing to work for Disney Studios until the idea was abandoned.

71.   Walt was upset by the strike, as he thought that he had always treated his employees fairly.

72.   The US government got involved and while Walt was out of the country they ended the dispute by giving in to the strikers' demands.

The War and After

73. The United States declared war on Japan in December 1941, after the bombing of the American naval base at Pearl Harbor. Disney was asked by the US government to make a series of training films for the Army, as well as cartoons to bolster the morale of the American public.

74. The war years were difficult for the Disney Studios, but when the fighting ended in 1945, Walt delivered more successful feature-length cartoons including "Cinderella," "Peter Pan," "Alice in Wonderland," and "Lady and the Tramp."

75. Disney also branched out into live-action movies with "Treasure Island" and "20,000 Leagues Under the Sea," and the studio began to thrive again.

76. The 1950s saw the rise of television, which many thought would keep people away from the movies. But Disney embraced this new technology, with Walt himself hosting his own weekly TV shows.

Disneyland

77.   Walt Disney was now a powerful figure in the entertainment business and had made enough money to begin his latest ambitious project – "Disneyland."

78.   Walt had dreamed for some time of creating a fantasy land where both adults and children could have a magical day out and meet all the Disney characters.

79.   Disneyland opened in July 1955, and people from all over the world flocked there to experience Walt Disney's dream come true.

80.   The opening day did not go according to plan though. It was an incredibly hot summer's day and the water fountains didn't work. Food ran out and there was a gas leak. The problems were fixed though and Disneyland became a great success.

81.   During the next decade Disney Studios made over fifty more movies, including classics such as "101 Dalmatians" and "Mary Poppins."

82.   The next big thing for Walt was a larger version of Disneyland, and work began on a new theme park in Florida. "Disney World" would be a theme park like no other, celebrating human achievement and ingenuity.

Walt Disney's Death

83.   Walt was not to live to see the opening of Disney World. He had been a heavy smoker since his time in France during World War One, and in 1966, he was diagnosed with lung cancer.

84.   He was told by doctors that he had less than two years to live, but despite this shocking news, Walt was cheerful and optimistic until the end. On December 15, 1966, Walt Disney died at the age of just sixty-five.

Walt Disney's star on the Hollywood Walk of Fame

Conclusion

To this day, the Disney Company still brings pleasure to millions of people from all over the world and it will surely continue to do so for many years to come.

Although Walt Disney is no longer with us, the company he founded continues to flourish. It has grown astonishingly since those early beginnings into an enormous multinational corporation worth billions of dollars. But as Walt Disney himself once said:

"I hope we'll never lose sight of one thing - that it was all started by a mouse!"

Illustration Attributions

Title page
NASA [Public domain]

Flora & Elias Disney
K10wnsta [Public domain]

McKinley High School
{{PD-1923}}

Made in the USA
Monee, IL
01 November 2021